Mary Arden's I
&
The Shakespeare Countryside Museum

Described by DR LEVI FOX, O.B.E., M.A., F.S.A.
The Director of the Shakespeare Birthplace Trust

Jarrold Colour Publications, Norwich in association with
the Shakespeare Birthplace Trust
Stratford-upon-Avon, England

Mary Arden's House

Of all the properties associated with William Shakespeare and his family, Mary Arden's House at Wilmcote, the home of the poet's mother, is probably the least known and yet in many ways the most fascinating. This Tudor farmstead, with its old farm buildings, was occupied and used for its original purpose until 1930, when the Shakespeare Birthplace Trust purchased it for preservation as a national memorial. It is situated just over three miles from Stratford-upon-Avon.

Standing back slightly from the roadway leading to the centre of the village, behind a wall enclosing quaint, shaped hedges of box, the timbered frontage of the house, as illustrated here, is of striking size and proportions. Most of the building is of early sixteenth-century date. The outer walls are of substantial oak timber framing standing on a stone foundation about three feet from the ground. The timber came from the wooded area known as the Forest of Arden nearby (mentioned by Shakespeare in *As You Like It*) and the blue-grey stone was quarried at Wilmcote, only a short distance away. At the front the upright timbers or studs are set close together, but at the back the framing is at wider intervals, forming large panels which were originally filled in with clay on a wattle foundation and coated with lime plaster. The roof, with its picturesque dormer windows with leaded lights, is covered with hand-made clay tiles.

It is most fortunate that continued occupation of the Arden farmstead by farmers ensured its preservation substantially in its original condition. As might be expected, minor alterations and improvements were made from time to time, but basically there has been no change in the layout and structure of the farm premises from Shakespeare's day to the present.

The plan of the farmhouse consists of a central passage or entrance lobby, with doors at both front and back, dividing the kitchen on one side from the hall, which served as the principal living apartment, on the other side. Originally open from floor to the raftered roof, the hall was subsequently converted into two storeys by the insertion of a floor supported by a massive oak beam, thus making possible a bedroom above. Later, another wing was added and used as the servants' quarters at the farther end. In other respects the house bears all the characteristics of the home of a yeoman farmer of comfortable status in Shakespeare's day.

At the rear of the house, a stretch of grass, with borders of herbaceous flowers and an oak tree planted to commemorate the Festival of Britain in 1951, occupies the space of the original farmyard, surrounded by the barns, stable, cowshed, dovecote and outbuildings preserved intact. The view of the farmhouse from here *(see next page)* is extremely fine, the combination of grey stone, bleached oak timbers and weathered red brick and tile harmonising perfectly with the simple, unspoiled country setting.

The Arden family

The Ardens, who lived here in the sixteenth century, came of an old and leading county family. Robert Arden was a prosperous farmer. He owned substantial land in the village of Snitterfield, near Stratford, as well as his farm at Wilmcote, which was known then as 'Ashbyes'.

Robert Arden's will directed that he should be buried at nearby Aston Cantlow church. When, shortly before his death, his daughter Mary married John Shakespeare, the wedding probably took place in this church. The eldest and third child of the marriage was William Shakespeare.

After Robert Arden's death in 1556 an inventory of his possessions was taken. The list shows the main contents and stock of Robert's farmstead to have included a variety of furniture, comprising tables, forms, benches, coffers and cupboards; beds, bedding, linen and painted cloths (used as wall hangings); copper pans, brass pots, candlesticks and cooking utensils; and a quern, kneading trough and vessels for milking and brewing. Also mentioned were various tools and farming implements such as ploughs, harrows and carts; wheat and straw in the barns; and livestock (oxen, cows, horses, sheep and pigs), as well as bees and poultry. All this estate was valued at £77 11s. 10d. Such was the background of the Arden farmstead and the early years of Shakespeare's mother.

Mary was the youngest of Robert Arden's family of eight daughters. When Robert died he left her in his will, besides money, his Wilmcote estate called 'Ashbyes', with 'the crop upon the ground sown and tilled as it was'.

The size of Mary Arden's House and the extent of its outbuildings, including a dovecote, show it was a family farmstead of considerable importance.

Entrance to the farmhouse is from the rear, as shown in this picture. On the right of the passage is the KITCHEN, with its paved stone floor and small leaded windows. Though now presenting a tidy appearance, with polished furniture and cooking utensils, this must have been a busy, sometimes untidy room where food was prepared and cooked for the family. Meat was roasted on the spit which revolved over the open fire in the large hearth and other food was cooked in a variety of pots and containers. Originally there was a bake-oven alongside, used for baking the family's bread.

On the opposite side of the passage is the GREAT HALL, which was the principal living apartment and the focus of the family's everyday life. Architecturally it has great character and over the years it has suffered little change, except for the insertion of a floor to carry a bedroom above. The foundation walls and floor paving are of the local Wilmcote stone. The roughly hewn beams and studding of seasoned oak give an impression of solidity and strength, and the small leaded-light windows allow shafts of light to illuminate a spacious interior. Lighting after dark was formerly provided by rushlights and candles, while the sole form of heating was from a log fire in the open hearth.

The hall is furnished with original pieces of furniture made by country craftsmen and similar to those which Mary Arden would have recognised. The tall-backed settle, dining table, joint-stools and court-cupboard, together with a variety of smaller items and utensils, recreate the atmosphere of domestic life in Tudor times.

Leading from the hall is the DAIRY with its sunken floor, containing milk pails and butter- and cheese-making utensils. This served as a cool place before the days of refrigeration. The SERVANTS' ROOM beyond is furnished in simple country style, with a table, benches and a coffer for storage.

The Shakespeare Countryside Museum

When the Trustees of Shakespeare's Birthplace acquired Mary Arden's House they decided that the barns and outbuildings around the farmyard provided an ideal setting for the display of old farming implements and tools, which, together with other domestic items, illustrate many aspects of rural life in Shakespeare's Warwickshire from Tudor times to the twentieth century.

Over a period of some fifty years a unique farming collection has been built up, partly by purchase and by gift, and the acquisition of the Glebe Farm has now made possible a comprehensive Shakespeare Countryside Museum,

utilising the accommodation and setting of two similar adjacent properties.

The museum is infinitely varied in its scope, but in general comprises all kinds of implements and tools of husbandry, utensils and domestic articles formerly to be found in farms and cottages, together with items illustrative of other aspects of country life such as crafts, communications, sport and pastimes. Some of the exhibits are very old, going back as far as Shakespeare's time; others are of more recent date, but perpetuating older types. They have one characteristic in common in that they provide a physical link with the life of the folk who have peopled the Warwickshire countryside in successive generations.

The farmyard

The area of grass at the back of the house occupies the space of the original farmyard, surrounded by the barns, stable, cowsheds, dovecote and outbuildings. Poultry, pigs and other animals were allowed to roam free and the yard was often covered with mud and manure.

As with many farmsteads in Shakespeare country, Mary Arden's had a CIDER MILL *(right)* for making cider from apples.

The DOVECOTE or pigeon house *(above)*, with 657 nesting holes, is evidence of the status of the Arden family, because the keeping of pigeons was restricted to the lord of the manor.

Inside the farmhouse

These illustrations of the KITCHEN *(bottom left)*, and DAIRY *(below)*, the GREAT HALL *(top left)* and SERVANTS' ROOM *(above)* give an excellent impression of the character of a Tudor farmstead. To walk through these rooms is like taking an excursion into the past. Only the members of the Arden family are missing.

A peep upstairs
The bare simplicity of the rooms upstairs emphasises the solidity of the oak timber framing and raftered roof. As shown in this picture of a bedroom on the left, roughly shaped trees were used for the principal beams and the framework was jointed and fastened together with wooden pegs.

The stable
Until the advent of mechanisation, the horse provided the motive power required for all farming operations other than those performed by oxen or manual labour. The STABLE with harness and provision for the horse can be seen in the picture above.

THE FARMING YEAR

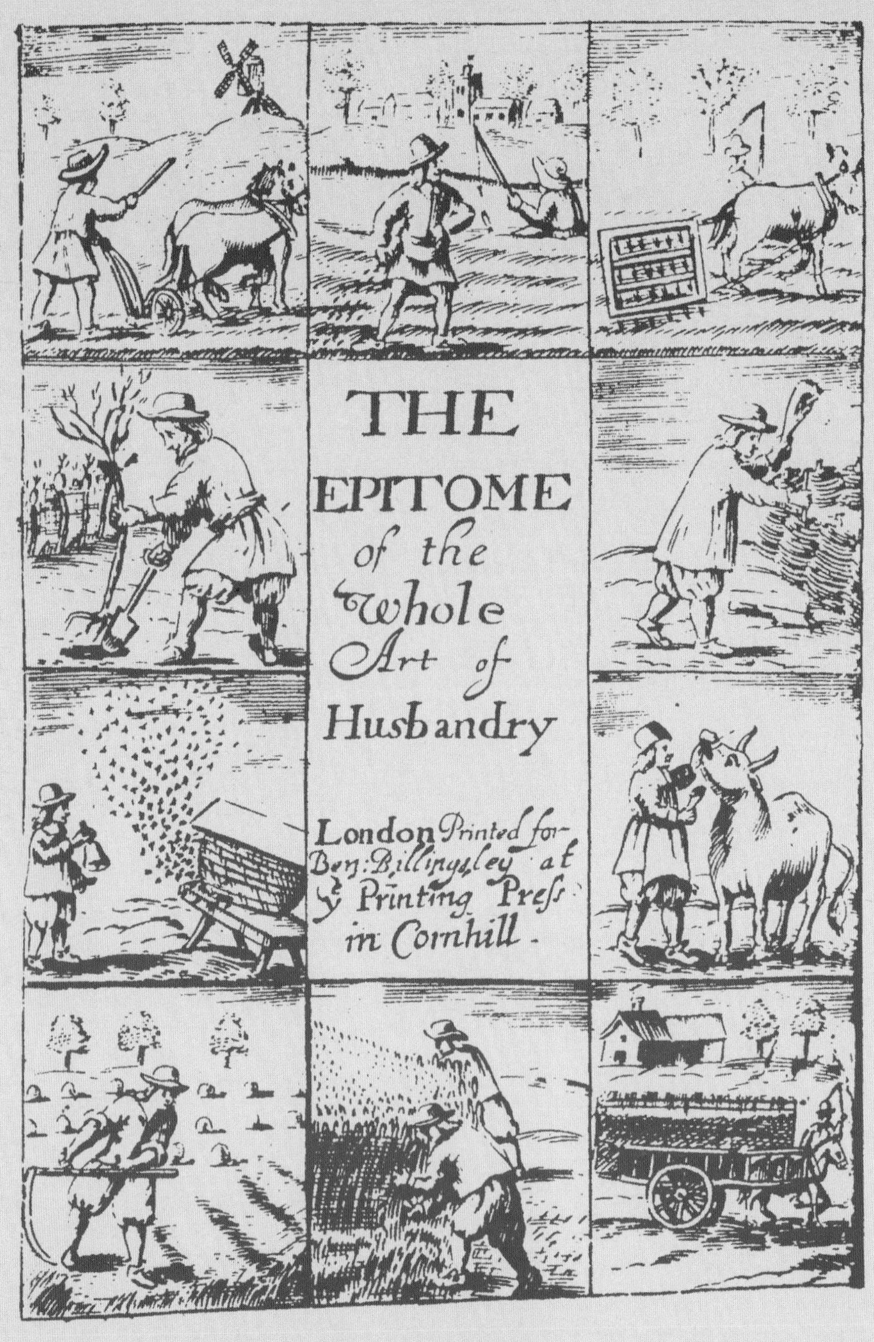

Published in 1669.

The spacious barns at Mary Arden's provide an ideal setting for displays like these, illustrating the farming year. Although many of the farm tools are of later date, they would have been recognisable to a Tudor farmer, and with the help of descriptive commentary and period woodcut pictures, they are arranged to portray the tasks the farmer undertook in autumn, winter, spring and summer. In winter the land was ploughed in readiness for sowing. Haymaking and sheep-shearing were summer tasks.

Mary Arde
The Shakespeare C

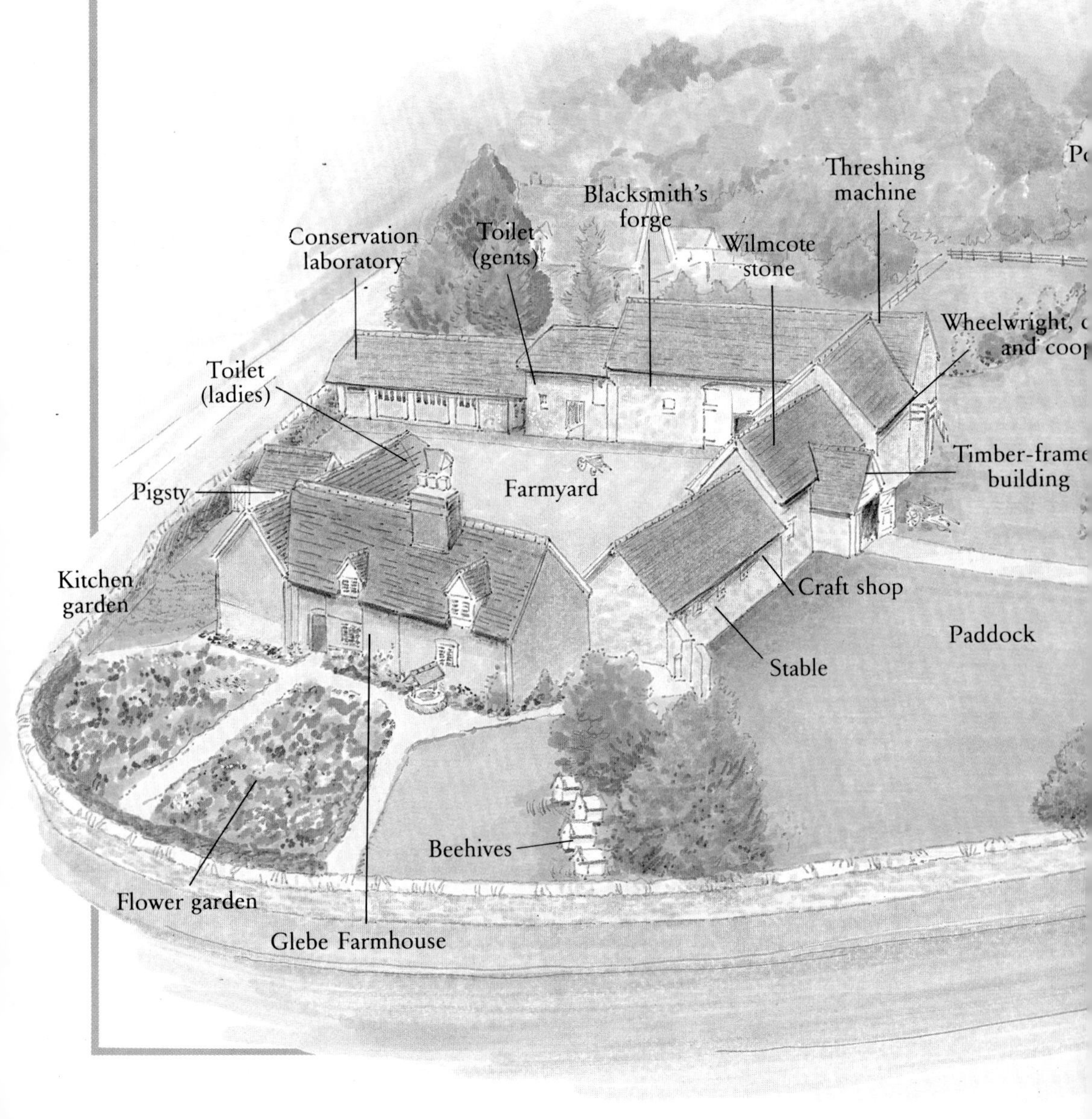

House & untryside Museum

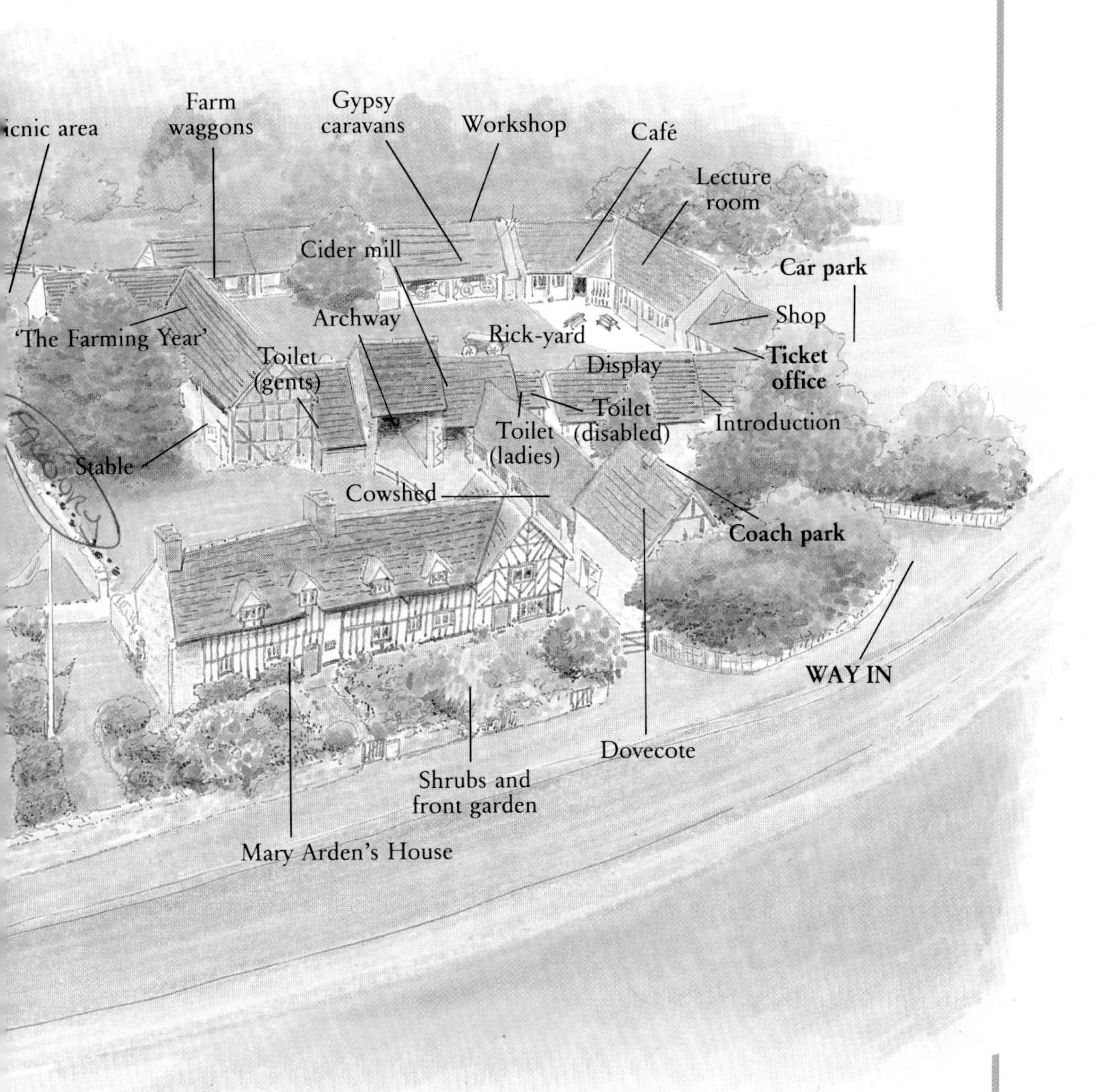

The Glebe Farm

The Glebe Farm, so-called because it originally formed part of the glebe lands belonging to the church, occupies a site opposite the village green within a few yards of Mary Arden's House.

So far as is known, this farmstead never had any connection with the Arden property, but evidence provided by the structure of the building substantiates that it was there in Shakespeare's time, when Wilmcote comprised only a few farm dwellings. It continued to be occupied as a farm until 1968, when it was purchased by the Shakespeare Birthplace Trust. Subsequently, the farmhouse and outbuildings were restored and they are now linked with Mary Arden's House and used to accommodate part of the Shakespeare Countryside Museum.

The earliest part of the Glebe farmhouse dates to the sixteenth century and was of a plan similar to its larger neighbour, Mary Arden's House. Originally, it consisted of a single main hall, open from floor to roof, built on a foundation of Wilmcote stone, and of timber-framed construction. As happened to the Arden farmhouse, the open hall was converted at an early date into two storeys by the insertion of a floor carrying a bedroom above. This explains why the ceiling of the living room as now presented is so low. At the same time, timber-framed wings were built on both sides of the hall to provide additional accommodation.

The Glebe farmhouse has suffered considerable alterations and adaptations to meet changing needs over the years. The front elevation has been largely re-faced in brick and much of the timber framing at ground-floor level has been removed; yet upstairs most of the original timberwork, with its wattle and daub panels, remains intact. An early twentieth-century iron range has been inserted in the original open hearth and the chimney-stack above the roof has been renewed in brick. Similarly, the bake-oven was discarded and bricked up when no longer required.

The walled plot in front of the house is laid out and planted as a typical country garden with vegetables, fruit trees, herbs, and a mixture of old-fashioned flowers and shrubs. Wells at the front and back of the house provided the water supply.

The stone barns and outbuildings are of similar age and type to those at Mary Arden's House.

The gravelled area at the back of the house was the farmyard around which stood the barns, stable and cowsheds, with a pigsty and granary approached by steps.

Inside the Glebe Farm

These illustrations give a good impression of the character of the rooms inside the Glebe farmhouse. The furnishings are typical of those commonly in use in the early years of the present century and many of the individual pieces are examples of country craftsmanship.

The LIVING ROOM *(top right)* is simply furnished with a large working table, chairs and a dresser displaying plates and storage jars, and a child's high chair *(left)*. The PARLOUR *(below)*, used for special occasions, contains a few family heirlooms and comfortable chairs in contrast to the KITCHEN *(bottom right)*. The setting portrays a washday in the early 1900s.

15

The basic pattern of country life changed little from Shakespeare's time to the early years of the present century. Life in a farmhouse was always busy, because the family was to a large extent self-supporting. The farmer's wife was well trained in all aspects of domestic management. In the picture opposite she is presented as an elderly lady, wearing an old-fashioned sun-bonnet, sitting by the table plucking a chicken.

The making of butter and cheese were regular tasks and the well-equipped DAIRY *(above)* was an essential part of the farmhouse. Facing east, it has thick walls and small windows which helped to maintain a cool, even temperature. Similarly, the sunken STORE *(right)*, with its cold stone slab provided ideal conditions for keeping game and perishable goods.

Country crafts

For centuries the BLACKSMITH was an indispensable craftsman. His regular task was to shoe horses (now undertaken by the farrier), but in this forge *(top right)* he also made all the wrought-iron tools and implements needed for the farm, the house and by other craftsmen.

Equally, the carpenter, wheelwright and cooper made vital contributions to rural life. Apart from the construction of buildings, the CARPENTER made tools, furniture and domestic items, as well as coffins, and acted as undertaker. His workshop *(centre right)* contained an amazing variety of tools, as did also that of the COOPER, whose speciality was the making of barrels of different shapes and sizes for the storage of beer, cider, wine and dry goods such as flour, salt fish, lime and crockery. The WHEELWRIGHT used a lathe and special tools *(bottom right)* to make and repair waggons, carts and other farm implements. Seasoned elm, oak and ash were used for the hub, spokes and felloes (curved pieces) of a wheel.

Wilmcote stone

This display of stone-quarrying and the mason's craft *(above)* is a reminder that the stone used in the construction of Mary Arden's House, the Glebe Farm and the outbuildings was quarried within a short distance of the site. Wilmcote stone was also widely used for paving slabs and in the manufacture of lime and cement.

Timber-framed construction

Oak from the Forest of Arden was the other basic material used in the construction of buildings in the Shakespeare countryside from the fifteenth to the seventeenth centuries. As shown in this display *(left)*, the carpenter fashioned roughly-hewn timber to make a framework, which was pegged together, ready to stand on top of the stone foundation walls.

The rick-yard

This area of grass, approached through the archway from the farmyard, was the rick-yard. It was originally unenclosed on three sides, the open-fronted hovels or sheds having been constructed by the Trust to accommodate and display farm waggons and other implements.

It was here that, following harvest, ricks of hay and corn were built on a framework resting on staddle stones, similar to the ones still on the site. This arrangement was used to deter vermin from climbing into the ricks.

A typical rick-yard scene usually included waggons, ploughs and other implements of husbandry left around when not in use. Free-range poultry, and sometimes pigs, roamed at large and cows, sheep and horses were never far away.

At the far end of the rick-yard, behind the great barn, a pond fed by water running down a ditch from the adjoining field provided a natural home for ducks and other wildlife.

Gypsies, or travellers, have frequented the Shakespeare countryside from Tudor times. These two CARAVANS *(right)*, built by Bill Wright, are of designs known as the Ledge and the Bowtop, the latter being the most typical Romany waggon.

Before the advent of mechanisation, the four-wheeled FARM WAGGON *(left)* drawn by horses played a vital role at harvest time.

The wooden horse-drawn FIRE-ENGINE *(above)* was used to fight fires in Stratford and the surrounding countryside.